"Angel's poems are like walking through Paris on a summer night – full of love, loss and lust, they leave you moist, shivering and wanting more."

– Chris

"A bit of 'angel' and a bit of 'sauce', combined for a truly delectable read! Yummm."

– MGA

"One of those rare souls who can put into (few) words what many of us can only stutter, stammer, and attempt to say in under an hour.

"Your poetry is romantic, beautiful, erotic, succinct, and causes the rest of us to think about the person we love. And smile. And for that I thank you.

"The world needs more poets like you."

– Jeff

"Insightful, colorful. I always enjoy the read!"

– Brian

Temple of the Soul

A Book of Poetry

Angel Woolery

Copyright © 2017 by Angel Woolery

All rights reserved.

No part of this book may be used or reproduced in any manner whatsoever without prior written permission of the author except in the case of brief quotations embodied in critical articles or reviews.

Editor: Courtenay Dodds www.courtenaydodds.com

Printed in the United States of America.

ISBN: 0692827005
ISBN-13: 978-0692827000

A broken heart pieced together is stained glass
in the temple of the soul.

DEDICATION

This is for you, my dear friends. The ones who cheer me on and push me, who muse me and love me, and nearly destroy me in moments of carelessness, but always save me just in time. The friends I trust with my heart and my sanity. Those of you who never stop believing in me. You who make me feel alive. I love you. I appreciate you more than you will ever know. I am a lucky girl.

Special thank you to Micah of MicahJTphotos, the sweet and wonderful Larisa, and my scrumptious cupcake Lorie.

Table of Contents

Unwritten	1
Haiku	3
Mask	5
Gravity of Love	6
Haiku	10
This Gift	12
Adrift	13
Haiku	16
In the Rain	18
Moonflower	20
Haiku	21
My Dear Friend	24
Growing Old	26
Always in the Quiet	27
Haiku	34
Never Would I Whisper	36

On Display	38
I Am Here	39
Silently	42
Haiku	43
Fate	45
I Closed My Eyes	47
Sasha	49
Destiny	51
Rooted in You	56
Haiku	61
Love Decided	63
Treasured	66
Haiku	69
Love	72
Elemental Play	73
Sisters	75
A Love Poem	77

Unwritten

I am untouched.
Unafraid.
At your whim.

I am right where you'd have me:
Splayed out before you,
a willing sacrifice.
As much at your mercy as you are at mine.

Wordless, I beg you to fill me.

Your hands gather me reverently.
Lowering your face to my center
as you breathe in my intoxicating promise.

My ivory pages stir eagerly
under your regard.

Angel Woolery

I see the promise in your eyes:
No longer will I languish unwritten.
You will fill me with words.

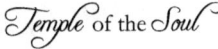

I did not see it
This part of you that charms me
Glad it's not too late

Angel Woolery

The taste of your skin
salty, damp, stirs her hunger
She devours you whole

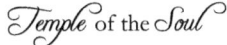

Mask

A lowered mask helps one to see.
My eyes on you,
your eyes on me.
For all that hiding makes us brave,
it's honest truth that we crave.
Bare yourself.
To hell with pride.
You are most wonderful
from inside.

Angel Woolery

Gravity of Love

Innocuous is how
she desired her visit to be
as she embarked upon
that day trip
through his soul.
She resolved to traverse
his tender feelings
as lightly as she was able.
Expecting,
even as she took such care,
that bruising was
inevitable.
The ache to caress
the source of his admiration,
overwhelmed any sense
she might employ.
And needing
just once

to bathe in the purity
of his affection,
she mouthed a silent apology
and immersed herself
in his warmth.
He held still his racing heart
mid beat,
not wanting to startle her.
His breath paused
awaiting her judgment
as painful moments of uncertainty
consumed him.
A lifetime of wanting
balanced on the perilous edge
of her acceptance,
far from his reach.
Never would this lady
have known
what his heart held
had she not trespassed.
Never would he have
braved an invitation.
He, ever at her mercy.
She, now unwittingly at his.
Surrounded by
the sheer intensity
of his regard,

Angel Woolery

she had never felt
so vulnerable.
His whispered yearnings
became a part of her
as they bypassed her ears
to slip through the hairline cracks
of her neglect.
Raw honesty
chipping delicately
at her defenses
'til they lay in ruins
at her feet.
A pile of useless assurance.
She had noticed naught
until 'twas far too late.
Attempting a hasty escape,
her footfalls only serve to
churn unexplored emotions,
like autumn leaves in
a late season storm.
And her
the mightiest of Oaks
taken by surprise,
finds herself bared
without consent.
Left exposed
by the most elemental of forces.

Temple of the *Soul*

Her once sure steps falter
as she struggles
to find purchase.
Knowing
he cannot let her fall,
he must let go his insecurities
to grant the safety
of his embrace.
She surrenders
to the inevitable,
and in the yielding
of willfulness
finds the key to her survival.
Acceptance.
The brilliance
such freedom of emotion
fills her with
serves to light her path
through eternity,
no longer trying to escape
the gravity of love.

Rain down upon me
Head tips, eyes close, storm clouds break
Soak me through and through

Temple of the Soul

Whispered promises
so hellishly hot, they are
a breath of kindness

This Gift

This gift I give you
is yours to do with as you wish.
If you treat it carelessly,
if you break it,
it is no business of mine.

What matter that it be my heart?

Temple of the *Soul*

Adrift

Cast adrift

Unwanted

Drowning
in
the melancholy
waves of my
despair

I choke
on each attempt
to breathe
your fluid lies

Sputtering my
disbelief

Gasping from

Angel Woolery

the force with which

you
deliver
your
imagined truth

Pain
steals
each
hard
won
breath

as I fight
to keep afloat

Struggling

against the current
of your contradictions

Faith,
my weakness

My belief,
eternal

Grasping

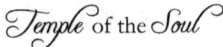

at the anchor
of you

Your worn steel
abrades me

Betrays me

Pulls me down

Your safety,
my demise.

Frustration is swift
Fiercely attacking resolve
that melts like sugar

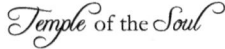

I leaned in too close
Anticipation weakens
In the mood for you

In the Rain

I tipped this aged visage
toward eternity

Broken
Imploring the heavens

Open

in answer to
an old friend
thirsty for redemption

The remedy
rains down timeless,

true.

Soothes my
tattered reality

Temple of the Soul

Returns to me my dreams

Each healing splash
blends seamlessly with
my tears
as they slide through the furrowed wisdom
I have bought
with my pain

With my soul

Heeding my sorrow
Restoring me
so that I may once again

run

unhindered in rain

Moonflower

Make haste!
Oh,
wretched night!

I've desperate need
of you

to coax these
dew laden petals
with your whispers

open

open...

Their heady fragrance
begs release
ere the arrival
of the sun

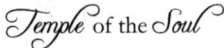 Temple of the Soul

Dew dampened petals
opening toward the sun
Sweet nectar exposed

Angel Woolery

Surrounded by dusk
Sunlight lingers on the air
We dream together

Temple of the *Soul*

Silently, I long
With sunlight comes emptiness
Warm pillow, no you

My Dear Friend

My dear friend,

I received your letters.

Each and every one.

I only wish I'd held them close
ere my time was done.

While my hands, they lay in stillness,
the pages seemingly unread
and my eyes could not caress your words
my heart served me instead.

I felt your friendship keenly.

I've fashioned my reply.

I postmarked it in eternity.

It reads:

My dear friend,
Goodbye.

Growing Old

In the corners of my mind
the cobwebs hang.
I hear only the echoes
of songs I've sang.
Only the shadows do I see,
faded memories of how it used to be.

In the mirror,
the reflection is no longer mine.
All I see is someone silenced by time.
My hands lay still
as I have no one to hold,
because I grew alone
as I grew old.

Temple of the Soul

Always in the Quiet

Always

in

the

quiet

When the night

is

black

as

pitch

My breathing

slow

and

Angel Woolery

even

Dreams

dreamt

deep and rich

Worries
left 'til sunrise

Trusting
sleep to keep me
safe

He calls
when I'm most
vulnerable,
this insubstantial
wraith

Eyes
snap wide
with knowledge
that I am
not
alone

I

Temple of the Soul

peer intently

into

darkness

heart racing

with unknown

I did not hear

a

footstep

or the creaking

of the floor

nor the gentle,

rattled

turning

of

the knob

upon my door

I tense

with

such

anxiety

though I feel

no fear

as ghostly fingers

run

along my neck

and

he whispers in my ear,

"My dear, do you remember me?"

Oh,

how could I forget?

Flooded daily

with

the memories

of a loss,

left me bereft

"I sorrow still," I tell him.

My

heart

bled out

its life

when his soul

left

mortal world

When this husband
left
his wife

These words seem
to bring him
peace

For how long,
I could not say

My love
is
his
eternally

I'll help him
find
his way

A sweet kiss
is
placed
upon my brow

then he
is

no more

I did not
hear
his footsteps

nor,
the creaking
of the floor

My weary head
lies soft upon
a pillow
warmed with tears
of woe
Exhaustion giving way
Eyes flutter
gently
closed

Always

in

the

quiet

When the night

is

black

as pitch

My breathing

slow

and

even

Dreams

dreamt

deep and rich

Moonlight bathes your face
Fulfilling me, becomes you
Tousled hair, I sleep

Temple of the *Soul*

Sweet upon my lips
a sticky, molten filling
My guilty pleasure

Never Would I Whisper

I must speak to you
my silence.

Words
never
ever
would I whisper
if not a soul would hear.

Free of discovery.
Protected from censure.
Safe.

Yet,
being words,
they clamor against constraint.
Begging to be uttered.

Temple of the Soul

Spilling forth
like silken hair
found suddenly
unrestrained.

Contrary to my wishes,
your acquaintance
they would make.

Shadowed nuance I let escape
to ease the burden of emotion
too keenly felt.

Still I will not speak.
If you would know them,
their introduction must be made
upon a page.

On Display

My consciousness on display for you.

Unadorned. Undisguised.
Exposed.

Your judgment,
like the blinding desert sun,
beats down upon me.

Merciless.

I do not cower under the attack.

I brazen out your silent derision.
Soles blistering on the blacktop of your scorn.

My soul.

My consciousness on display for you.

I Am Here

HELLO?

DO YOU SEE ME?

I am right fucking here, and yet
you have passed me by
for what seems the millionth time
with no hint of recognition.

There is no:
How are you?
Is everything good?
I miss you.
I need you.
I am sorry.

No:

Thank you for being there always for me.
Ever for me.
Nothing.
And I am right fucking here,

seemingly invisible to you.

Lonely.
Unnecessary.
Forsaken.

I do not even feel discarded.
I am not that important.

Not anymore.

I am simply forgotten.

Intentionally.

You never promised a single thing.

I stupidly believed in words
you did not speak.

I believed in you.
Foolishly.
In us.

I am bereft.

Eyes red from withheld tears
and
swollen from those that escaped in
an avalanche of misery.

My voice barely a whisper now
so tired am I.

From hoping.
From trying.
From loving you.

I am right fucking here.

Silently

It's fascinating that a heart
can break so silently.
With nary a whisper,
it lies crumbled at your feet.
Love,
the glue that held it all together.
Loneliness,
its absolute defeat.

Temple of the *Soul*

I see you truly
No mask hides your intention
Still, you are my friend

Sweet dreams you wish me
My mind holds you through the night
Dreams so sweet I ache

Fate

Had you never graced this earth,
ne'er would your Fate exist.
Your dreams would pass unrealized.
Your potential lost to mist.

Rain could not caress your face
to wash away the tears.
Laugh lines would never frame those eyes
to testify your years.

Your love would wander aimlessly
in an ether so unkind,
unfulfilled for all eternity:
The beauty of your mind.

No solace could you offer,
if you never were.
No home to fill with happiness.
No heartache to endure.

Sunshine would never warm your flesh.
No child would you hold.
On no lover could you bestow your touch,
if ever you felt bold.

All colors merely shades of gray
without you to set them free.
A sweet voice condemned to silence
cannot sing life's melody.

But Fate has secrets not revealed,
your story still unfolds.
You'll write the final draft yourself
as Fate is yours to mold.

I Closed My Eyes

I took a breath, closed my eyes,
I nearly had control!
My feelings overtook me.
What grip I had let go.

Never one for holding back,
my abandon is perfected.
Jeopardy, a siren song
and I, left unprotected.

This free fall took an eternity.
It happened in a blink.
Perhaps I'm perched upon the edge
always on the brink.

The descent, I look back fondly,
was filled with happy sighs.
Wind rushed by exhilarating.
I gave some lusty cries!

Angel Woolery

I was unafraid of toppling over.
I flung myself quite hard!
The freedom filled me up complete.
Intense was my reward!

Cascading clarity, I'm unrestrained.
This tumble took its toll.
It's a good thing I know how to land.
I always tuck and roll!

Sasha

I yearn alone
amongst the heavens.
My whisper extends
to caress her soul.

But softly.

Gently.

I've no wish as yet
to end the enchantment
mere mortals feel within her gaze.

She is the magic of creation.

The wonder of stardust.

She is everything.

She is nothing.

She is.

I've no intent to let her go.

I,
the one who set her free.

For, in all of her,
is every part of me.

Temple of the *Soul*

Destiny

You

are

a

force

over which,
I have no control.

You lead me
doggedly
down a path,

toward an end

I cannot foresee.

My eyes kept wide,

still the mystery remains.

Be it
the path of virtue?

Is it wrought of
primrose?

It is of no import.

I must
follow.

I am
susceptible
to you.

Your slightest whim
compels me.

Your softest whisper,
my command.

When you hold back
nothing,

I am your casualty.

My heart left
in a million

Temple of the *Soul*

jagged,

tragic,

little pieces.

But when you love me,

when
you
really
love
me,

your gentleness
is
my undoing.

Your caprice can find me

Spent
from passion

or

bathed in anguish.

You care not
how I receive
your will

as long as you are the brace
upon which I arc.

So,

I will let you
have your way with me

more times
than seems prudent.

I can do no differently.

You are as certain
as moonlight.
As inescapable
as life.

Destiny.

Without you
I cease to exist.

You are both
rogue
and
cherished friend.

Your caustic wit
oft

sears me.

Your generosity,
sweet
balsam.

I trust you.

I must
be
mad.

Rooted in You

So many lifetimes have passed since last we met.
Countless battles lost in crushing defeat.
Exhilarating triumphs we could not share.

Lifetimes, where your absence was felt keenly.

Long,
lonely lifetimes
spent restlessly wondering what was amiss.

Completeness, a concept just beyond my reach.

You see,
I have no memory of you.
No mementos
tucked away
in a pretty little box.
No faded, ribbon wrapped letters to hold to my heart.

Temple of the Soul

And, while I cannot quite recall

a single word from

songs we've sang,

the melody of you

resonates

within

me.

All our whispered dreams.

Our hopes.

Desires.

Fears.

Spoken in the dark stillness of a thousand winters,

while we awaited spring.

These are the tendrils of our existence that seek to bind us

together,

again

and

again

and again.

Our shared secrets.

The content

long lost to us.

But still,

I'd never tell.

Only the confidence remains.

You are my friend.

Ever

and

always.

You are my friend.

Even now,

when there is nothing left of you and I,

but a colorful,

comfortable feeling

woven deeply through the fabric of

time.

I know, I never want to leave your side.

I never would.

Never willingly.

Never,

ever

quietly.

My wishes to remain are

oft times ignored by capricious gods.

They are fools to think we will not find each other.

Temple of the Soul

In the times between us,
there are wonders aplenty.
Yet nothing as wondrous as you.

I do not need you to fill some imagined void.
The thought alone is blasphemy.
Your absence itself
is a void I must fill.

No finite memory exists.
Still, I remember you.

What is memory anyway, but a collection of feelings,
and sounds,
and tastes
returned to haunt us?
To tickle.
To tempt.
To invite renewal of a friendship so old,
time forgot to end it.

Somehow, I remember you.

Intuition most basic,
it does not submit
to reason.

Love never did.

And you my friend,
I will love for eternity.

When you are present,
and
when you are not.

With lashes lowered
Your manly form is admired
Covetous woman

Angel Woolery

Without you, I ache
Fingers taste of completion
Need overwhelmed me

Love Decided

"I don't want you to fall in love with me."
"It's too late," he said.
"I cannot ever let you go.
Lie back upon the bed."

Powerless to stop him
Unwilling to even try
She let his need recline her
He was emboldened by her sighs

His eyes held her regard
She could not look away
So many years she'd wandered searching
waiting for this day

A man, so overcome with her
he loved her desperately
If she would simply cease protest
and allow the ecstasy

Angel Woolery

She'd not be disappointed
by the promise in his touch
He'd take a million years to please her
if she required such

His caresses ever gentle
as his lips rained their assault
Her need was so intensified
No one would find fault

That wanting, weakened her resistance
Would have brought her to her knees
Had his hands not been busy parting them
to drink from in between

Single-minded in his task
She, completely drenched
By the time she surrendered all
his thirst still wasn't quenched

His hands began their worship
as he inhaled her scent
He was quite intoxicated
with this lover he'd been sent

From the soles of her feet
to her love-mussed hair
he savored every part of her

Temple of the Soul

'til he could no longer bear

To be separate from her body
while immersed inside her soul
He slid into her tightness
His savagery let go

No longer gentle was his passion
as she welcomed him to feed
Upon her freely offered love
as he filled her with his seed

Their cries were heard in heaven
as new love was given birth
Two lovers twined in sated bliss
as they settled back to earth

Treasured

You've held me safely in your heart;
a warm memory of a kinder year.

A more innocent time.

A time of heat,
of youth,
of impetuosity and recklessness.

And you still think of me as perfection.

You

think

of

me.

And I like it.

Perhaps I am wrong to do so.

Temple of the Soul

That will not stop me.

It's not like I have a choice.

Your words romance me.
Unsettle me.

Make me uncomfortable.

In a way I would never voice.
In a way that makes me blush.

You have not forgotten the way.

I cannot look at what might have been.
Not with the stark realities of life
swirling around.

Not on a mundane,
otherwise uneventful day.

Your memory, I savor.

I cherish.

I cannot forget.

I will peek at the dark end of day, under the soft acceptance of
the pale moonlight, where you remain a smile on my lips.

A sigh

of restlessness
inhabiting my soul.

I will hold you safely in my heart;
a warm memory of a kinder year.

A more innocent time.

A time of heat,
of youth,
of impetuosity and recklessness.

I will still think of you.

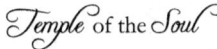

Cupped by greedy hands
Quenching far more than mere thirst
Partake thoroughly

Fresh from completion
your scent still upon my skin
I am your hostage

Temple of the Soul

Pleasure will not wait
Left to my own devices
I keep you in mind

Love

Love.
The only gift
you can give
that fills the heart,
eases the mind,
satisfies the body,
and lightens the soul.

Temple of the *Soul*

································

"Way, way, way back I was a random assortment of elements swirling through space trying to get myself together...at least I am not flying through space anymore." ~Patrick~

Thank you for your inspiration.

I see you dispersed.

I should gather you.
All your pieces.
Admire you to whole,
though the beauty
of you elemental
is a sight.

Your flow of raw power
courses through me,
like neutrinos on
their journey.

It fills me with delights.
Does not weigh me down.
Warms the very core of this soul.

Do I gather you?
Contain you?
Or, shall I watch the dance?

Free,
you span the entirety,
kicking up dust in your play.
How did you come to such a state?

I think I will recline
in Ambartsumian's Knot
and enjoy your design.
I will take each moment
and savor, until such a time as
you feel you must collect yourself.

Temple of the *Soul*

Sisters

Together.
You and I
e'er since
the dawn of time.
Forever.
I am yours.
Always.
You are mine.
Blood lines
are inconstant.
Genders, they reverse.
In some lives
I am the eldest.
In others,
you're the first.
My allegiance
will not falter.
On your side

I'll ever be.
Love stands
as reassurance.
Mine for you.
Yours for me.
My loss would
be complete
and I,
beyond repair,
should I find
I need a hand
to hold
and my sister's
not be there.

Temple of the *Soul*

A Love Poem

I'd have you know that love surrounds you.

In your deepest despair
and your greatest triumphs,
you are not alone.

Never
alone.

At times you may not be able to see through your pain
and your pride may hide its truth.
Yet it is there.
If you could but take a peek,
you'll discover you were not once left adrift.
Someone's hand was extended,
inviting you to reach.

Just reach.

It is evident in the kind words of a stranger

Angel Woolery

and the laughter of friends.

In the unending willingness of man to help his fellow man.

It can arrive,

a whisper on a warm breeze

or in a torrent

of emotion.

The good in the world is overwhelming.

The simplicity of love is stunning.

Its expressions innumerable.

It can embrace you in your darkest hour

and encourage you to greatness.

It is quiet acceptance.

You do not need to ask for it.

You do not need to feel worthy of it.

It is already yours.

You are loved.

You

are

love.

Temple of the Soul

Angel Woolery

Angel Woolery's published works include:

The Taste of Innocence – A Book of Poetry

Waitress: a memoir

and as a contributing author in:

Behind The Veil
On The Verge
Into The Abyss

All available on Amazon.com.

Angel would love to hear from on you on the web:

Facebook Page: Angel Woolery – Writer
Facebook Page: Angel Woolery – Poet

www.ingramcontent.com/pod-product-compliance
Lightning Source LLC
Chambersburg PA
CBHW071317040426
42444CB00009B/2034